REMARKABLE EXPERTS

Vol. 2

REMARKABLE EXPERTS

Vol. 2

Spotlights on Leading Authorities and Professionals

LEADING AUTHORITIES AND PROFESSIONALS

FEATURING:

Corina Freitas
Fletcher Ellingson
George Platt
Marc Haygood
Sean Duffy
Adam Skuba

Remarkable Experts Vol. 2/ Mark Imperial —1st ed.
Managing Editor/ Shannon Buritz

ISBN: 978-1-954757-09-7

Remarkable Press™

Royalties from the retail sales of **"REMARKABLE EXPERTS Vol. 2: SPOTLIGHTS ON LEADING AUTHORITIES AND PROFESSIONALS"** are donated to the Global Autism Project:

The Global Autism Project 501(C)3 is a nonprofit organization that provides training to local individuals in evidence-based practice for individuals with autism.

The Global Autism Project believes that every child has the ability to learn, and their potential should not be limited by geographical bounds.

The Global Autism Project seeks to eliminate the disparity in service provision seen around the world by providing high-quality training to individuals providing services in their local community. This training is made sustainable through regular training trips and contiguous remote training.

You can learn more about the Global Autism Project and make direct donations by visiting **GlobalAutismProject.org.**

Contents

A Note to the Reader

Thank you for buying your copy of "REMARKABLE EXPERTS Vol. 2: Spotlights on Leading Authorities and Professionals." This book was originally created as a series of live interviews; that's why it reads like a series of conversations, rather than a traditional book that talks at you.

I wanted you to feel as though the participants and I are talking with you, much like a close friend or relative, and felt that creating the material this way would make it easier for you to grasp the topics and put them to use quickly, rather than wading through hundreds of pages.

So relax, grab a pen and paper, take notes, and get ready to learn some fascinating insights from our Remarkable Experts.

Warmest regards,

Mark Imperial

Publisher, Author, and Radio Personality

Introduction

"REMARKABLE EXPERTS Vol. 2: Spotlights on Leading Authorities and Professionals" is a collaborative book series featuring leading professionals from across the country.

Remarkable Press™ would like to extend a heartfelt thank you to all participants who took the time to submit their chapter and offer their support in becoming ambassadors for this project.

100% of the royalties from this book's retail sales will be donated to the Global Autism Project. Should you want to make a direct donation, visit their website at GlobalAutismProject.org

CORINA FREITAS

CONVERSATION WITH CORINA FREITAS

Corina, you are the founder of Freitas & Associates. Tell us about your business and the people you help.

Corina Freitas: Forensic psychiatrists mainly work with counties, jails, law enforcement, and lawyers. We are at the interface of our field (psychiatry) and the legal field. Similar to Forensic accounting being at the interface between the law and accounting/financing or how Forensic medicine deals with medical reasons for death and the law, forensic psychiatry focuses on mental health and the law. We do a lot of work within the court system.

What is the most common type of work that you do?

Corina Freitas: Everyone is very enthralled when they hear that I'm a forensic psychiatrist. They say, "Oh, please tell me about all of the murderers you get to talk to and demystify or profile." But it's really not as glamorous as Hollywood portrays it. A lot of the work we do involves competency to stand trial. We also do independent medical evaluations for people who have trouble at work or in other arenas. Perhaps they experienced trauma or something that was hindering them from working at their full capacity. So the most common things we do are much more civil than the glorified Hollywood "I'm going to meet Charles Manson tomorrow" type of work.

Can you give us an example of a case?

Corina Freitas: A common criminal case is when someone goes to court for any particular reason; if they are disruptive or appear not to understand what is going on, a judge will order what is called "competency to stand trial." We then come in as forensic psychiatrists and interview the defendant to try and determine if they can understand the court proceedings. If we decide that they can't, we have to have a reason. Just because they aren't competent doesn't mean they have a mental illness. And on the other side, just because they have a mental illness does not mean they are incompetent.

A common civil case would be an assessment for fitness for duty to return to work in some capacity or another. For example, a police officer or a nurse returning to work after severe trauma significantly impacted their mental health.

Besides forensic psychiatric evaluations, what is something unusual that professionals in your field could help with?

Corina Freitas: Forensic psychiatry can help in so many ways, including legal advocacy and public policy formation. Other ways in which we can help are trial preparation or attorney file review of medical records. Also, we can offer lectures for CLEs and more. But we also can consult for fun things! We can consult with TV and movie producers, novel writers, the news, and so on!

Do you handle many insanity pleas?

Corina Freitas: Cases like that are very uncommon. Statistics show that only about 1% of defendants try to go the route of "not guilty by reason of insanity." And even less than that are actually successful. It's more of a movie thing. But in a situation where that does occur, we would conduct a very similar evaluation. People often think that just because they have a history of mental illness, they can plead not guilty by reason of insanity. But that is not necessarily true. We have to look at the facts and determine if they are truly psychotic, manic, or whatever it is they were claiming to be at the time of the crime. A clinical psychiatrist only gets to look at the patient in front of them and take that at face value, developing opinions based on conversations. However, as forensic psychiatrists, we have the luxury of police records, mental health records for the past 20 years, and crime scene behavior and information. So we can give a good timeline and can say, “Well, this patient has been psychotic 20 times in the past, and this is how it looked. They’re telling me that the period of psychosis that caused them to commit this crime was completely different than normal.” So we take that into context and what the crime scene looked like, behavior at the crime, and behavior after the crime. Then we can argue whether it is probable or not that they were actually mentally ill at the time of the crime.

What inspired you to become a forensic psychiatrist?

Corina Freitas: My mom always tells a funny story. I'm not sure how true it is, but she says that ever since I was four years old, I would say to her I wanted to know what was going on in people's heads. I've always been drawn to the military and police, as my father was a Navy captain and my grandfather was a criminal prosecutor. So I believe I have a bit of genetics or influence from the family in that regard. I've grown from family medicine to psychiatry to forensic psychiatry through the years, trying to marry all of my academic loves.

How do people find a forensic psychiatrist when they need one?

Corina Freitas: Forensic psychiatrists are everywhere. Few of us practice forensic psychiatry as a full-time job because we need to maintain our clinical acumen. So most of us practice clinically in some form or another, and we have this hidden talent of being a forensic psychiatrist. A lot of it is by word of mouth. Also, if you're a member of the Forensic

Psychiatry Association, you can find people there. But the most important avenue is by word of mouth.

How can people find you, connect with you, and learn more?

Corina Freitas: My website is freitasforensics.com. You can also email me at freitasforensics@gmail.com. I can be reached by phone at 315-552-1667.

CORINA FREITAS

Founder, Freitas & Associates

Dr. Freitas is dually boarded by the American Board of Family Medicine *and* the American Board of Psychiatry and Neurology. She is actively engaged in the practice of both clinical psychiatry and medicine. She has been qualified and testified as an expert witness in the states of NY and VA.

Dr. Freitas serves on the Council of the American Academy of Psychiatry and the Law and is an active member of several committees: Addiction, Law Enforcement Liaison, Forensic Services Liaison, and a founding member of the Women's Committee.

Dr. Freitas' past experiences include working as a Medical Attending providing emergency services, as a Telepsychiatrist providing addiction services, as well as serving on Quality, Housestaff, Advocacy, and Ethics Committees.

Dr. Freitas is also an active member of the American Academy of Addiction Psychiatry, American Psychiatric Association, and the American Academy of Forensic Sciences, where she has presented at national conferences.

- **WEBSITE:**
  www.freitasforensics.com
- **PHONE:**
  315-552-1667
- **EMAIL:**
  freitasforensics@gmail.com

- **FACEBOOK:**
  https://www.facebook.com/freitasforensics

- **LINKEDIN:**
  https://www.linkedin.com/company/freitasforensics

FLETCHER ELLINGSON

CONVERSATION WITH FLETCHER ELLINGSON

Fletcher, you are the founder of The Practice of Feeling Good. Tell us about your business and the people you help.

Fletcher Ellingson: I have several types of clients I work with, but my main focus is entrepreneurs. Now more than ever, people are out there surviving instead of thriving. I empower entrepreneurs to shift from financial uncertainty to predictable income, from overwhelm to clarity, and from worry to confidence, so they can get back to what they love doing and contribute to their families and communities.

Especially during the pandemic, people are experiencing challenges. What are some common concerns you are hearing from clients?

Fletcher Ellingson: Uncertainty is a massive concern right now. One of the six human needs that Tony Robbins talks about is the need for certainty. There has been so much uncertainty and unpredictability that people are scrambling for control because they feel out of control. One of the things that I help my clients do is surrender the need for control and learn how to trust that life is working out for them now, help them see that it always has worked out, and trust that it always will. The incredible thing is that when we give up our fear and surrender our desperate attempt to control, the floodgates of creativity and possibility open up for us. My clients report a sense of being in the zone, and things just start lining up. We engage our brains differently when we feel good, and by good, I mean safe, certain, secure, happy, creative, etc. I believe that people want to feel good above all else. It's why we want family, money, health, experiences, and all the toys that we buy. It's also why we contribute and why we want to make an impact. All of these things have the potential to help us feel good. And I believe that the practice of feeling good absolutely has the power to transform our lives and our planet. But the KEY is to realize that all the external things that help us feel good are temporary. When we learn to feel good inside as a result of the practice, all of the external things we have been chasing simply magnify how we already feel inside. It's a beautiful thing to watch and experience.

Tell us about your methodology.

Fletcher Ellingson: We're focused on three areas of life: health, wealth, and relationships. Those three areas make up our lives. I'm not big on strategies, and I'll tell you why. We have more strategies than we can shake a stick at. All of my clients already have strategies they know they *should* be using. But they say, "Fletcher, I know what I *should* be doing, but I'm not doing it. And I don't know why I'm not doing it." Giving them more strategies would only compound their challenge and frustration. So we set the strategies aside and instead focus on rewiring the brain and nervous system. I'll give you an example. Three ladies I worked with had type 2 diabetes. They were depressed, overweight, had high blood pressure, and were at risk for other severe health complications. They already knew that they *should* eat a healthier diet, and they knew they *should* be exercising. What they didn't know was why they couldn't implement and stick to a healthier lifestyle. They were extremely frustrated, unhappy, and resigned. What they learned through my program was how to rewire their brain and nervous system, which allowed them to interrupt old dis-empowering habits and set up new empowering habits that allowed them to navigate life with greater ease and joy. The result was that they all lost weight, lowered their blood pressure and blood sugar, came off many of their medications, and....wait for it... they all completed their first-ever triathlon after 12 months of working on their mindset. And one of the women was 70 years old!

Albert Einstein said, "We cannot solve our problems with the same level of thinking that created them." So I help people think differently. If you want to get a radical result in your life, you've got to do two things. Number one, you have to radically change the way your nervous system is responding. And you've got to radically change your literal thoughts. Brain scientists say we have about 60,000 thoughts a day. And the alarming thing is that all of those thoughts are the same ones you had the previous day, the previous week, month, year, and so on. So you aren't really learning anything new. To learn something new, you have to change how you are processing information and bring massive intention to it. *And that is core to The Practice of Feeling Good.*

What inspired you to start The Practice of Feeling Good?

Fletcher Ellingson: From an early age, two things were of significant interest to me. Personal development and business. In fact, in elementary school, I was reading Norman Vincent Peale's book, The Power of Positive Thinking. I remember my dad thought that was particularly odd! Since I was in sixth grade, I've also been an entrepreneur, delivering papers, mowing lawns, and washing windows. I've always been an entrepreneur. So I guess from very early on, I was destined to be helping people transform their personal and business lives.

At one point, I had a manufacturing and sales business that I was highly passionate about, but it crashed and burned because I was missing the fundamental key: mindset. I don't just mean positive thinking. When I really began to tap into mindset and understand how the brain and nervous system worked together, I interacted with my business very differently. I was able to build a multimillion-dollar business and speak all over the country. I began studying with some of the top minds in the personal development space. And finally, I came up with my own methodology as a result of having wonderful mentors. Now I am working with people all over the country, and it's spectacularly fun. My clients are creating incredible results!

I'll give you an example. Barb was a client who was continually stopped by fear when she would think about reaching out to a potential client to inquire about helping him list his home. She had been putting it off for months. She had lots of good reasons, but in the end, they were all excuses masking her fear. After a one-hour conversation, we uncovered her fear and replaced it with confidence and an inspiring vision. She then was able to get into action, called the person, and as a result, listed the home and eventually collected a $35,000 commission. That's what is possible when we evolve our thinking. So let's put that in perspective. A one-hour phone call resulted in a $35,000 commission. Pretty cool!

Can you give us another example of the results some of your clients see from going through your program?

Fletcher Ellingson: You bet. Some of my clients have kicked their addiction to drugs and alcohol. One of my clients, Tim, is an incredible young man. He was fresh out of the military and was in a dark place. A couple of his military friends had committed suicide. He even had some thoughts of suicide. He was drinking too much and didn't have much in the way of savings. After diving into the mindset work, he kicked his addiction, landed a high-paying job, and began building up his savings. Then he went back to college, completed his degree, began volunteering in the community, and is loving life! Those kinds of results really are priceless!

Then there is Meg, who was a photographer who really wanted to move from hobby to business. Her issue was she just didn't believe it was possible. She didn't know where her clients would come from, and she was terrified of selling. After learning how to manage her thinking and think differently, her confidence blossomed. Within four months, she had clients who were raving about her work, had landed high-profile long-term contracts, and was off the charts happy and inspired.

It's all about the practice of feeling good. When we feel good about ourselves, we have access to flow or being in the "zone." When we feel good, we have access to progress. And progress begets progress, and then we experience momentum. And, of course, momentum feels good, and now we have created a cycle of feeling good! When that happens, life begins to look and feel magical!

Can you tell us more about what you mean by the practice of feeling good?

Fletcher Ellingson: Absolutely. Think about people in the medical field, such as physicians, nurses, and PAs. They practice medicine. A lot of what they do is pattern recognition. They look at a condition or situation and consider it against a bank of information that allows them to make a diagnosis. If they step away from their practice for a significant time, they may find themselves a bit rusty upon their return. They may need to brush up and review certain information and techniques that once had come easily to them because they had been so practiced. The same goes for attorneys. They practice law, and if they stop for a time, their skills can become diminished.

For 30 years, I have been a performing magician. I love watching and performing close-up magic. It requires consistent practice on a daily or at least weekly basis. There have been times when I stopped practicing, and it does not take long for me to notice that my execution is not nearly as sharp. Consistent practice is required.

People at the top of their game, such as Tiger Woods, Simone Biles, and David Blaine, excel at their crafts because they are always practicing. They don't ever think, "Oh, I can stop practicing now." No way, they have coaches and mentors to help them take their practice to the next level.

It's the same for you and me, no matter what our profession. We are practiced at the way we speak and interact with people, and we are especially practiced at the way we think. Consider that we very rarely bring attention to our thoughts. Instead, our thoughts just show up. We have snap judgments about people based on beliefs, most of which we did not intentionally choose. We adopted similar thinking to the thinking of our parents or our instructors or the media, etc.

Then we became very practiced at those thoughts meaning, that we thought those thoughts over and over until they became a program in our brain. For instance, if we had a frightening experience with a dog when we were young, we may grow up with a fear of dogs. We may have thinking that says, "Dogs are mean, scary, and can't be trusted." And we have thought that thought so many times that we have become practiced, and we don't question whether it is accurate or not because the thought happens automatically. We have these thoughts about every single area of our life. We have automatic thinking around our health, wealth, and finances. We get upset because we are practiced at getting upset. We feel insecure or shame because we are practiced at it. We can also feel confident, resourceful, and capable due to practicing those ways of being.

What I help my clients understand is that it takes practice to feel good. Most people are practiced at feeling upset, cynical, resigned, angry, frustrated, etc. Then these ways actually become part of their character. We say things like, "She is such an angry person."

I want people to know that they can feel good, meaning secure, fulfilled, enthusiastic, open, willing, trusting, happy, eager, to name just a few. They can feel these ways more of the time and even on-demand! And it takes practice. So I have my clients do very specific activities in the course, resulting in them actually thinking differently about their lives. Their brain processes data differently than it used to. They are intentional about how they want to feel about life. They become practiced at bringing empowering and feel-good stories to their everyday life. This is actual transformation. What I mean by that is they are interacting with life in a way they simply did not have access to before. They have successfully created new neuropathways in their brain that are being used on a regular basis. And when this happens, they have access to results that were not previously possible.

Now, a word of caution here. If these new pathways are not used on a regular basis, they will just pare apart. The practice of noticing life working out is a daily practice. The practice of intentional gratitude, meditation, defining ourselves, overcoming fear of rejection, and disappearing shame and guilt are just a few examples of the practice.

Again, this is not just positive thinking. The entire curriculum is approximately 12 months and entails weekly sessions because we are committed to off-the-chart results. This is for people who want radical results!

How can people connect with you and learn more?

Fletcher Ellingson: You can go to fletcherellingson.com or thepracticeoffeelinggood.com. Peruse the website. There are several free resources. You can schedule a free discovery call on the website. It's an hour-long call, and this is not a hardcore sales call. It is to find out what challenges you are facing, where you feel stuck, and to find out if we are a good match and if I can help you. If you're stuck or feel like you have plateaued in your relationships or business, let's have a conversation. There are solutions out there. You don't need to suffer, and you can move forward powerfully.

FLETCHER ELLINGSON

Founder, The Practice of Feeling Good

Fletcher Ellingson is a coach, speaker, entrepreneur, and founder of Ellingson Enterprises, a coaching and training company. He helps other entrepreneurs break free from financial struggle, management overwhelm, and persistent worry so they can spend more time doing what they love, contribute to their families, and make an impact in their communities. Fletcher has studied with some of the best minds in the personal development industry. In addition to over 25 years of speaking and performing for audiences across the United States, he and his wife, Dr. Amy Ellingson, host a weekly television show addressing topics of health, wealth, and relationships.

- **WEBSITE:**
  www.fletcherellingson.com
  www.thepracticeoffeelinggood.com

GEORGE PLATT

CONVERSATION WITH GEORGE PLATT

George, you are the VP of Sales and Marketing for GHP Media Inc. Tell us about your business and the people you help.

George Platt: GHP Media is in West Haven, Connecticut. We have 140 people over three shifts of production, and we're in the printing and direct mail business. GHP covers 12 different avatars, from financial services to nonprofits. I tend to work with manufacturers, higher education, direct marketers, information marketers, and people in private practice. So I basically use printing and direct mail to grow people's businesses.

What are the biggest challenges you help your clients overcome?

George Platt: Most people don't realize their customer list is the biggest asset they have, and it's right under their nose! Many people aren't doing anything with their customer prospect list. It's really a crime. Most businesses get in the trap of only being an expert in doing their business. But when you are doing the marketing for a company, you have to be in the marketing business. You're just the marketer of what you do, not the doer of what you do. So I work very closely with people to help them get their business growing again.

Are there misconceptions that keep people from taking advantage of their databases?

George Platt: Many people think direct mail is dead. I do a lot of work with non-profits, colleges, and universities. With the big push toward digital spending, they abandoned their annual reports and stopped printing them. They just put them online in PDF format or on their website. But people want to see their name in print; they want to flip a page and find their name. So business went way down for people who abandoned print and direct mail. Many big retailers did the same thing. They ended up realizing they had made huge mistakes when they stopped printing their catalogs.

Well, it's like jumping into a crowded digital space. And now the mailbox is relatively empty, right?

George Platt: That's the beauty of doing direct mail. 70% of people go to the mailbox and get their mail. And of those people, 68% are actually opening it and reacting to it. So it's still more powerful than ever.

Are there other big mistakes that manufacturers or information marketers are making to hinder success?

George Platt: They just stop marketing. When COVID hit, people just stopped marketing and spending money when it should have been the other way around. Another mistake is thinking they are direct mail experts. They say, "Well, what's the legitimate percentage of response?" The response rate has something to do with it, but it's the wrong approach. They should be asking, "What is the lifetime value of my client?" If you have a lifetime value of clients that have spent 20 million dollars with you over your career, what would you take out of your wallet to buy one of those clients? You have to look at marketing and direct mail spend as an elegant way to buy clients. My mentor Dan Kennedy would say, "If you can afford to spend the most to buy a client, you're going to win." Marketing and advertising should be looked at as investments, not expenses. Another thing people say is, "I'm going to budget 5% of my sales on marketing." But if a media will pay its way, throw the budget out the window! As long as it is self-sustaining, spend all the money you can.

George, what is the state of direct mail today versus other digital marketing initiatives?

George Platt: Give "snail mail" the respect it deserves. Critics will say that in the 21st century, other methods of communication are more popular than physical mail. There are email and texting and Facebook ads. And then, on top of that, we hear nothing but bad news about the state of the Post Office and how it's losing money.

It's funny, though. Despite what they say, the Post Office's business is in direct mail. Let's look at the specific advantages that direct mail offers over every other form of product promotion.

I've put together a list of just some of the ways that direct mail marketing is your best choice. Keep this list handy, and if you ever start to wonder whether direct mail is right for you and worth the expense, read this list to refresh your memory:

There's Less Competition These Days for Your Prospect's Attention

The critics have one thing right. In general, people are mailing much less frequently than they used to. Instead of writing letters, people are emailing, texting, and using Facebook.

But what does that mean for your direct mail campaign?

For one thing, it means that advertising by sending an email is not your best bet. People's inboxes are filled to the gills, so nothing stands out, and many messages go directly into a junk folder.

It also means that when people pick up their physical mail, there isn't as much to distract them from YOUR message. In fact, there's a greater likelihood these days that a direct mail sales piece will be read than even a few years ago.

And statistics show that the vast majority of people pick up their mail and read it right away. Plus, they actually have a measurable positive emotional response to physical mail.

So, with less competition for their attention and positive anticipation, your prospects will gladly read your sales piece.

It's the Closest Thing to Talking Over the Kitchen Table

The world today is overloaded with distractions. When we watch television, we're bombarded with commercials. Does any one commercial really stand out in the string of five or six commercials that are aired during the commercial breaks?

And then, as I mentioned, there are all those emails clogging inboxes or ending up in the junk folder. If your ad were part of that deluge of messages, can you be sure that you'll be noticed? Research shows that the open rates for email are declining, and it's getting more difficult to make online sales. So that may not be the best way to try to get your message across.

But what happens when a person opens your sales piece and sits down with it? You've got that person all to yourself. No other ads are interfering with your prospect's attention. No emails are coming in to pull them away.

It's like you're sitting at the kitchen table with them, explaining that you understand their problems and needs, promising them that you have the perfect solution, and telling them the simple steps they should take to get their hands on the answer to all their troubles.

It's that one-on-one aspect of direct mail that makes it so powerful. Nothing can beat that.

You Can Home in on Your Best Prospects

When you put an ad on TV or in a magazine, you're just sending it out to the whole universe of people, but not all of them are going to be interested in your message. You really only want to get the attention of a small number of people who have a reason to want to learn about your product. It's a waste to blast away at everyone in general – with the danger that no one will notice – including your best prospects.

When you advertise through direct mail, you can be much more scientific in your approach. List sellers have a tremendous amount of information about the people on their lists. They have demographic details (age, gender, number of children, income level, geographic location), along with specific interests, health issues, and so on. That means that you can precisely target your most qualified prospects.

Your Buyers Are More Likely to Yield a High Lifetime Value

I've done a lot of research in this area based on my clients' results, and I have found that the buyers you attract through direct mail just end up spending more money and remaining more loyal over an extended period of time. That means that the reverberating effect of your direct mail efforts is to bring on continuing orders and increasing profits over time.

What I've done is to compare the lifetime value of three different kinds of customers based on how they were first introduced to various companies. Customers were generated through TV ads, online campaigns, and direct mail. What I found was that:

- Online buyers spent the least amount of money over time.
- The lifetime value of the TV buyers was double that of the online buyers.
- And – drumroll, please – the direct mail buyers had a lifetime value that was nearly double that of TV buyers and triple that of online buyers.

This clearly shows that direct mail is superior to other forms of advertising when it comes to pinpointing the right population of buyers and converting them to long-term customers with great lifetime value.

Keep all this in mind the next time you plan your advertising budget. Direct mail could well be the best use of your money.

What inspired you to get into direct mail and marketing?

George Platt: It sounds religious, but I'm about my father's business. My father started the printing business in 1955, and he ended up buying a printer in 1972. I went to college, got a degree in printing management, and went to work at the company in 1976. As I was beginning my career there, my father passed away in 1982. I have been running the business ever since. I'm a big believer that money should move; it shouldn't stay in one place. So I'm a 20% giver; I'm a double tither. Between church and charitable organizations, I keep the money moving. And the more I keep the money moving, the more it finds its way to me. My father had grown the business to $700,000 in sales, but when I took it over with my two brothers, we needed room to grow more. So I became a student of marketing and direct mail. I've spent $100,000 to $200,000 just educating myself throughout my career, and that is on top of college. When you have that competitive fire in you, you want to win. And that's what I do; I help people compete and win.

How do people find you, connect with you, and learn more?

George Platt: My email is george.platt@ghpmedia.com. You can reach me directly by phone at 203-479-7560. If you email me your name, snail mail address, and phone number, I have a book for you. It's a quick, easy 57-page book entitled "10 Big Secrets for Growing Your Business in the New Economy." If you send me an email requesting the book, I'll send it out to you free of charge. It highlights all of the marketing methods that have given me huge returns over the years. So this is $200,000 of investment and 45 years of testing all wrapped up into one book. So send me an email. I'll send it to you.

GEORGE PLATT

VP of Sales and Marketing
GHP Media Inc.

George has been President of The Harty Press, Inc since 1982. He and his brothers, Kevin and Michael, led Harty from under a million dollars in sales to over 20 million in its best year.

George was responsible for the strategy and execution of the marketing and sales side of the business. George is active in the Seventh-day Adventist Church in New Haven and is a board member and Treasurer of the church's school, Laurel Oaks Adventist School offering grades 1-8 in Hamden, CT.

He has held all leadership positions in Connecticut's printing industry associations. George served as the Industry Co-Chair of the Greater New Haven Postal Customer Council.

Harty was founded in 1900 and withstood many world wars and countless recessions. Harty was not able to survive Covid-19 and the following pandemic. In April 2020, George brought all his sales and most of his sales team to GHP Media Inc. in West Haven, CT. As Vice President of Sales & Marketing, George is responsible for the book of business that came from Harty and the marketing of GHP Media. GHP has highly talented people to offer you an extensive array of marketing services, including digital and offset printing, large format posters, banners, direct mail, and marketing communications. Your peace of mind is our main concern.

■ **WEBSITE:**
www.ghpmedia.com

■ **PHONE:**
203-479-7560

■ **EMAIL:**
george.platt@ghpmedia.com

MARC HAYGOOD

CONVERSATION WITH MARC HAYGOOD

Marc, you are an expert in holistic herbalism and nutrition. Tell us about your company, Ancestral Medicinals, and the people you help.

Marc Haygood: We carry many natural plant-based products, but we specialize in detoxification. Ancestral Medicinals caters to people who want to take a more proactive approach to their health or desire to make lifestyle changes to become more healthy. Our customer base is 80% women.

What are some common challenges that people face who are looking for holistic or herbal remedies?

Marc Haygood: Many people are frustrated about being overweight. With the times that we live in, people seek alternatives because conventional medicine does not focus on nutrition or the internal environment of keeping ourselves healthy. In addition, holistic treatments acknowledge the relationship between mind and body; the mind plays a major role in our health and well-being, which is often overlooked in western medicine.

What are some myths and misconceptions regarding holistic or herbal remedies?

Marc Haygood: People have been trusting doctors for a generation; we go to the doctor out of habit. Since people are so used to conventional medicine, it has a negative stigma when you mention herbal or alternative medicine. Modern medicine is less than 100 years old, and it often does not recognize other modes of healing that have been used successfully for generations. Due to the failure of modern medicine, the COVID pandemic, and overloaded hospitals, people are getting frustrated with modern medicine and are seeking alternatives. There are many people not only sick but overweight. Obesity is the number one challenge in our country right now. Almost 70% of people are overweight. The key is to acknowledge that we are responsible for our health.

What are some things people can do herbally to reduce obesity?

Marc Haygood: Most People are not overweight but "OVERWASTE," with poorly digested food and waste matter. The average American walks around with more than 20 pounds of this poorly digested waste material in their body.

Herbal and natural remedies focus on prevention. Don't wait until you have a problem; that is key. But once there is a problem, you have to change your lifestyle. It's not just about taking a pill, getting a shot, or signing up for a Zumba class. You have to change your *entire* lifestyle, including your mindset.

That is tough for people because they like to stay where they are. This is where our detox programs start, working on the cause, not just relieving the symptoms.

What are some mistakes people make to keep them from reaching their health goals?

Marc Haygood: People expected results yesterday. We live in a "get rich quick," "get healthy overnight" society. Most people would prefer to take a magic pill instead of putting in the work. In addition, people forget about nutrition. Many people do detoxes, but then they don't change their diet. With our detox, you have to eat an alkaline diet consisting of fruits and vegetables high in water. People are so used to eating heavy "acidic" foods that giving those up for a week to thirty days is very difficult for them. Also, we emphasize the mind because it plays a significant role in our health. We also help people detox the mind, letting go of things they have been holding on to or no longer serve them.

What are the benefits of detox?

Marc Haygood: Toxins are causing many of our problems. The term detox means to "rid of toxins." There is a difference between detoxification and cleansing. I think of it as spring and fall cleaning; these are done so your house doesn't get overloaded. Our typical detox is designed to reboot your system so your body does not get overloaded with toxins. Your liver is your main detoxification organ, but we focus on the whole body, not just the liver, but the kidneys, blood, lungs, skin, and lymphatic system. It's basically a reset for your body. We often recommend that people start with detox if they want to change their diet, battle chronic fatigue, high blood pressure, or other ailments. Clean your system and change your diet for a couple of weeks because sometimes, all it takes is a good flush of your system for things to reset automatically.

What inspired you to start Ancestral Medicinals?

Marc Haygood: Well, it was two things. First of all, my wife at the time had a cyst on her ovaries. We kept going to the doctor, they would give her antibiotics, and the cyst would just go away and come back. I was inspired to read about detox and potential ways that I could help her naturally. I put her on a 30-day detox, and the cyst ended up coming out in the toilet. It was black, covered in maggots and mold, and looked disgusting. But after that, she had no more problems. We had been going to the doctor for five years with no success or only temporary success. So being able to help her through my own research really inspired me.

Secondly, I live in a rural area; nature is everywhere around me. Just being in this natural environment enabled me to connect with plants on a deeper level.

How do people find you, connect with you, and learn more?

Marc Haygood: Due to COVID, we are doing a lot of remote work. We used to do detox classes in person but have shifted to electronic, phone, and Zoom correspondence. We offer a free 15-minute consultation for the first ten people to email us or visit our website at amed1.com. You can also give us a call or send a text to 708-844-1560. Now is the time to take responsibility for your own health.

MARC HAYGOOD

President and Founder
Ancestral Medicinals

Born to teach the world what life from the earth tastes like and how it can extend living naturally, Marc Haygood is a practicing Master herbalist and nutritionist. He is known as "The HERB DOC" with extensive knowledge of wild plants and trees, intrinsically bringing together original, natural, herbal remedies and modalities that revive, restore, and heal.

Holding a degree from the University of Notre Dame, he is the founding Principal of ANCESTRAL MEDICINALS, a holistic herbal remedy practice. Marc grows, makes, and packages his own line of herbal products and services.

A scholar, public speaker, and curator, he has created and hosted health seminars and herbal walking tours, appeared on cable access television and radio, provided health consultations, and written blogs and journal articles. He has redefined what it means to go outside, play, and get dirty for three decades. Inspired by the earth's unknowns, his studies have led him to answer some medical mysteries and complexities; through proven holistic approaches.

For more information, visit www.amed1.com or call 708-844-1560

WEBSITE:
www.amed1.com

PHONE:
708-844-1560

SEAN DUFFY

CONVERSATION WITH SEAN DUFFY

Sean, you are the Founder and President of Integrity Pharmacy Consultants. Tell us about your business and the people you help.

Sean Duffy: Integrity Pharmacy Consultants assists independent pharmacy owners that are exploring their options of selling. We provide information on the process, help them with valuation, and help them maximize the selling price when they are ready to sell. We do it all within the pharmacy industry. Everybody with our company; we're all pharmacists. And we've all got incredible experience with different aspects of the pharmacy industry.

What are some common challenges people face when selling their pharmacies?

Sean Duffy: Anybody who knows anything about pharmacies knows it's the reimbursements. The margins continue to erode year after year as insurance plans reduce reimbursement while the price of drugs increases. So it's leaving less margin for some of these independent owners to be successful. It's very challenging.

Are there myths or misconceptions that sabotage people from achieving success in selling?

Sean Duffy: The "one more year syndrome." They say, "I'll give it one more year to see if things get better." And then it's another year and another year. With the trends in the way pharmacy is moving, not only are independents losing margins on their profitability, but so are the larger chains buying the pharmacies like CVS, Walgreens, and Rite Aid. They are not offering as much as they once were to purchase your business. So the longer you wait, the less value you will have when it comes time to sell.

What are some common mistakes people make when selling their pharmacies?

Sean Duffy: Most owners don't know what the true value of their pharmacy really is. You have to know what point you can negotiate to. There are multiple aspects to the selling process that allow you to maximize profitability or reduce your tax liabilities once you sell. Most independents are concerned with how much money will end up in their retirement or savings account at the end of the day. And unless they have been through multiple different transactions to sell on a pharmacy, they will not know what pockets to negotiate and to what extent.

What inspired you to start Integrity Pharmacy Consultants?

Sean Duffy: When I was growing up, my father was an independent pharmacist. So I was a second-generation independent pharmacist. When I was in college, the pharmacy was sold to a big chain because they offered a whole suitcase full of cash to pay for the business, which I couldn't have even begun to do. So I ended up working for retail chains and made my way up into corporate management, to the point where I was actually involved with buying independent pharmacies, bringing them into our chains, and working with their files and inventories. I saw how much money these independents were leaving on the table. While I was working for the chains, my heart went out to the independents. It just killed me to see these owners in business for 30 to 40 years, leaving hundreds of thousands of dollars on the table because they didn't know what they needed to do. I decided to leave the retail chain environment and start this business to help independent owners through the process when the time came.

You have a really unique perspective from being on both sides of the transaction. Is there anything else you would like to share?

Sean Duffy: If you are selling your pharmacy, explore different options and talk to people who might help you, whether it is Integrity Pharmacy Consultants or someone else. You have to trust them. How long have they been helping owners sell pharmacies? How many pharmacies have they been involved with selling? What types of reviews do they have? Are they pharmacists with industry experience? Once you feel comfortable with someone and their level of expertise, you can feel confident about moving forward.

How can people find you, connect with you, and learn more?

Sean Duffy: Our website is integrity-rx.com. I'm always available on my cell at 480-855-3584. You can send me an email at sean@integrity-rx.com.

SEAN DUFFY

President and Founder
Integrity Pharmacy Consultants

Sean has 30+ years of retail pharmacy experience. Over the last several years, Sean has worked exclusively with independent pharmacies and small chain owners to help sell their pharmacies. He started Integrity Pharmacy Consultants to help independent owners as there are limited resources for knowledgeable and trusted Pharmacy Consultants/Brokers. His most gratifying accomplishments have been mentoring talented professionals, providing opportunities for others to succeed, and helping independent owners through the selling process. He is hardworking, honest, and lives by a high level of moral standard. When he is not working, he likes to road bike, mountain bike, watch Hawkeye sports and spend time with his wife and two kids.

- **WEBSITE:**
  integrity-rx.com
- **PHONE:**
  480-855-3584
- **EMAIL:**
  sean@integrity-rx.com

ADAM SKUBA

CONVERSATION WITH ADAM SKUBA

Adam, you are the founder of Skuba Entertainment. Tell us about your business and the people you serve.

Adam Skuba: I am a wedding DJ entertainer, serving the Poconos, Central Pennsylvania, and Northeast Pennsylvania areas. I have lived here my entire life. I supply one-of-a-kind entertainment for couples looking for more than a cookie-cutter wedding DJ. I sit down with them, plan everything out, and strive to give them an experience that is truly unique to them.

The wedding industry was turned upside down by the pandemic. What's happening in your neck of the woods currently?

Adam Skuba: Before the pandemic, we had many receptions that consisted of 150 to 200 people. That was probably the norm. Now couples are scaling back to around 100 guests but spending more money on original, creative elements. For example, hotel ballrooms are becoming a thing of the past. People are looking for more unique venues, upscale food and decorations, flowers, and entertainment. They are spending more on these aspects instead of the higher guest count. As an entertainer, that is really important because before it was a numbers game. You had 200 to 250 people, you played some music, and some people would dance, some people would not. With smaller groups, if half the guests leave right away, an empty dance floor doesn't look great in photos or make for a good time. These days, we need to be very in tune with what the couple desires to create a memorable experience for everyone.

It sounds like it is less about money now and more about the experience. Is this true?

Adam Skuba: The pandemic really shined a light on the value of memories and celebrations. There has been a great deal of loss for many families enduring the deaths of loved ones from Covid. These times of getting people together are more important than ever. So people want to make sure the celebration is memorable for all the *right* reasons, not the wrong ones.

Are there any new challenges people should be aware of when planning their weddings?

Adam Skuba: Absolutely. Many people are looking at alternative venues right now, such as barns. These venues may not be set up for a wedding the way country clubs and hotels are. And that's where my role as a master of ceremonies comes into play. I help craft a timeline and a "day-of" schedule for these couples. I showed up recently to do a wedding that was literally in the woods. I had to bring my own power. I had to bring my own table. I had to bring everything. The food people showed up, the photographer showed up, but there really wasn't a coordinator to help everyone flow as a cohesive unit. With my expertise and experience, I sent everyone a timeline in advance to plan out the reception. Everything went great, and the couple had a wonderful time. They said, "Without you taking the reins and keeping things moving, all of the guests probably would have eaten dinner and left." But I made sure to keep everyone involved and in tune with what was going on.

What is your role as a DJ entertainer?

Adam Skuba: When a wedding is done right, it looks seamless. When it goes wrong, it's a dumpster fire. I remember one wedding where the mother of the bride contacted me to book the whole thing. She expressed that the couple was really interested in a different setup. They wanted it to be in the woods. And I said, "OK, you need to start thinking about things like restrooms and lighting once it gets dark out there." I wanted to make sure the guests had a good time.

Sure, they could have gotten one of those battery-powered things from Walmart or Sam's Club and thrown some music on, but I was able to give them an experience. They had a piano player in the woods, and I was able to mic the piano. It was the piano that sat in the bride's grandmother's house for many years. Then I transitioned them into the cocktail hour, with the alternative music that the couple was interested in. I also transferred the guests to different areas of the woods for special events, like the first dance. With all of these added elements, music would have been such a tiny part. They could have called a DJ and said, "Hey, we need music in the woods." And maybe that would have happened. But I sat down with them and went through every detail, from getting power out there to working with other vendors. They were so appreciative of the entire thing. I should add, it was a dry wedding. This was a very conservative Christian family who chose the woods because it was right behind a church. The father of the groom was the pastor of this church. So this wasn't the typical "get drunk and fall down" type of wedding. They wanted something totally unique to them. And I think we accomplished it.

Are there any common myths and misconceptions in your industry?

Adam Skuba: Since we offer photo booth services in addition to our DJ entertainment, we are at many weddings that we are not providing the entertainment for if they just want the photo booth. One of the biggest things I see is people who hire a great DJ from their favorite bar or club. He is excellent at mixing music and spinning tunes. But everything comes to a screeching halt in terms of announcing the wedding party. I think the most important parts of the evening are the wedding party introductions and introducing myself to the guests. Some of these people fall flat on their faces when it comes to that. They can keep the dance floor rocking but fail to let everyone know what is going on through announcements.

A big misconception created during Covid was DJs spinning music over Twitch and Zoom, doing dance parties in their houses. And while it was entertaining, it didn't give couples a chance to see how they function on a microphone and perform in front of guests. That's why I always go back to saying, couples need to meet their prospective DJ face-to-face. That person is going to be representing the couple for the entire day. Nobody wants to watch a game show with a really lousy host.

Adam, you have been a Remarkable Expert in this industry for a long time. What inspired you to become a wedding entertainer?

Adam Skuba: I started when I was very young in my high school and college years. I was an announcer for a local professional wrestling group. Through that, I met people and started doing birthday parties and other events. A catering manager approached me and said, "Have you ever done a wedding before? It's like a birthday party, except you announce the names beforehand." I was only 15 or 16 years old at the time. I had never done a wedding but have come to find out through my career that there is A LOT more to it than what that lady told me.

I went to college for TV and radio production. I really enjoyed that, but interacting with people was what I enjoyed the most. Nothing beats seeing smiling faces and being around people having a good time. I knew I wanted to go out and entertain for couples. I learned as much as I could through workshops, conferences, and online resources about delivering the best experience to my clients. I'm still learning to this day. The day you stop learning is the day you stop living. I'm always looking to expand my knowledge base to give the absolute best to the couples I work with.

What are the most frequently asked questions from people who are first reaching out to you?

Adam Skuba: The first question is always, "How much do you charge? It doesn't matter what you do, how much do you charge?" I guess they just don't know what else to ask. Yes, price is important. Some people truly can only afford X, Y, and Z. On the other hand, many people don't even know what they are buying. As a DJ entertainer, it's important to position yourself and have your information out there so couples have a good feel for what you offer. I have a lot of online resources. Many couples come to me as direct referrals from weddings I have done previously. They might have a feel for what I do, but not the whole picture. I wrote a book called "Your Ultimate Wedding Reception," which takes couples through the process of asking the important questions to a potential wedding entertainer.

The next question is always, "Are you available for the date?" So maybe I'm cheap, but I'm not available. Or perhaps I'm available, but not cheap? I don't know. At any rate, I take that opportunity to educate the couple and ask some questions. "Did you think about the ceremony? What are you going to do for ceremony music? If you have cocktail hour in the downstairs area, how will you get sound down there? Would you like live musicians for that?" I network with many live musicians too, and we offer that service. Once the couple sees me map out the entire evening and all that's involved, they start to understand price a lot more, and we can have a great conversation about everything we can do.

What is your best piece of advice on how to choose the right DJ?

Adam Skuba: Do your homework. Meet face-to-face. Find out how much experience they have. Have them explain how they have made other couple's weddings shine and be memorable. And the answer shouldn't be, "Oh, we played a lot of music and rocked the dance floor." There is so much more to it than that. What exactly is your entertainer going to do to make the event unique to YOU?

How can people find you, connect with you, and learn more?

Adam Skuba: My website is www.skubaentertainment.com. You can reach me by phone at 570-450-6874 or on Facebook at Skuba Entertainment. I'll be more than happy to send a copy of my book to you and answer any questions you have. We can even set up a Zoom to go over details.

ADAM SKUBA

Owner, Skuba Entertainment

From a young age, music was a huge part of Adam's life. Instructed by his musician grandfather, Adam was out entertaining the community at only five years old!

While in high school, Adam started DJing birthday parties, senior citizen events, and even weddings! In a short time, he became a full-fledged business owner before graduating and moving on to college at Wilkes University. He realizes how lucky he is to have found his passion for music and business at such a young age and blend it into his full-time career.

With decades of experience in the wedding industry, Adam continues ongoing education in his field to learn more and stay ahead of the trends so he can always offer his couples the best experiences on their wedding day.

Adam has been featured in both Mobile Beat and DJ Times trade magazines, recognized as The Greater Hazleton Chamber of Commerce's Young Entrepreneur of the Year, a member of The Knot Hall Of Fame, and a consistent recipient of The Knot Best Of Weddings and Wedding Wire Couples Choice Awards.

- **WEBSITE:**
  SkubaEntertainment.com
- **EMAIL:**
  adam@skubaentertainment.com
- **INSTAGRAM:**
  skubaentertainment
- **FACEBOOK:**
  Facebook.com/Skubaentertainment
- **PHONE:**
  570-450-6874

About the Publisher

Mark Imperial is a Best-Selling Author, Syndicated Business Columnist, Syndicated Radio Host, and internationally recognized Stage, Screen, and Radio Host of numerous business shows spotlighting leading experts, entrepreneurs, and business celebrities.

His passion is to discover noteworthy business owners, professionals, experts, and leaders who do great work and share their stories and secrets to their success with the world on his syndicated radio program titled "Remarkable Radio."

Mark is also the media marketing strategist and voice

for some of the world's most famous brands. You can hear his voice over the airwaves weekly on Chicago radio and worldwide on iHeart Radio.

Mark is a Karate black belt, teaches kickboxing, loves Thai food, House Music, and his favorite TV shows are infomercials.

Learn more:

www.MarkImperial.com
www.ImperialAction.com
www.RemarkableRadioShow.com